Awesome African Animals!

A+
books

Meerkats Are Awesome!

by Lisa J. Amstutz

Consultant: Jackie Gai, DVM
Captive Wildlife Vet

raintree

a Capstone company — publishers for children

Raintree is an imprint of Capstone Global Library Limited, a company incorporated in England and Wales having its registered office at 7 Pilgrim Street, London, EC4V 6LB – Registered company number: 6695582

www.raintree.co.uk
myorders@raintree.co.uk

Edited by Mari Bolte and Erika Shores
Designed by Cynthia Della-Rovere
Picture research by Svetlana Zhurkin
Production by Morgan Walters
Printed and bound in China by Nordica.
0914/CA21401520

ISBN 978-1-406-28848-3
18 17 16 15 14
10 9 8 7 6 5 4 3 2 1

British Library Cataloguing in Publication Data
A full catalogue record for this book is available from the British Library.

Acknowledgements
Alamy: Adam Seward, 20 (bottom); Dreamstime: Alta Oosthuizen, 6, Manit321, 10, Schnappschusshelge, 16 (bottom); Getty Images: Barcroft Media/Burrard-Lucas, 13; iStockphotos: GlobalP, cover (top right), 1 (top), 18 (top); Minden Pictures: Vincent Grafhorst, 12; Newscom: Moonshine Media/Jeremy Jowell, 20—21, 22, Photoshot/NHPA/Martin Harvey, 28—29, Photoshot/NHPA/Nigel J. Dennis, 17, Robert Harding/Ann & Steve Toon, 26—27; Shutterstock: Aaron Amat, cover (top left, bottom), back cover, 1 (bottom), 32, Alfredo Cerra, 14, belizar, 19, Bildagentur Zoonar GmbH, 23, Black Sheep Media (grass), back cover and throughout, e2dan, 29 (bottom), EcoPrint, 16 (top), 25 (top), Fiona Ayerst, 8—9, Kristina Stasiuliene, 15, MartinMaritz, 25 (middle), Michael Wick, 24—25, Photodynamic, 5, santol, 11, spirit of America (African landscape background), throughout, Super Prin, 7 (back), Tina Rencelj, 18 (bottom), Tristan Tan, cover (top middle), 7 (front), 26 (middle), Valentyna Chukhlyebova, 4

We would like to thank Jackie Gai, DVM, for her invaluable help in the preparation of this book.

Contents

Living in Africa

Pop! A furry head pokes out of a hole. Then another, and another. Soon there's a whole mob ... of meerkats!

A meerkat is a mammal. It belongs to the mongoose family. It can measure up to 29 centimetres (11 inches) tall and weighs about 0.9 kilograms (2 pounds).

Meerkat fur is light brown with dark stripes. The fur matches the dry soil. Meerkats' fur hides them from predators. Dark rings around their eyes act like sunglasses in the bright sunshine.

Africa

Where Meerkats Live

Meerkats live on the plains of Africa. The ground is dry and rocky. Grasses and shrubs dot the land. The sun blazes hot. Summer days can reach 40 degrees Celsius (104 degrees Fahrenheit). It is hard to keep cool in Africa. But meerkats do a good job.

Meerkats pant like dogs to cool down. Their coats shed heat well. They dig up cool sand and lie on it. Or they cool off in their underground burrows.

Digging deep

Meerkats live in burrows. Sometimes they share them with other animals, such as ground squirrels or yellow mongooses.

Burrows are full of long, underground tunnels and rooms. The many exits are called bolt holes. Above ground, meerkats stay near these holes. They dive in when danger is near.

Meerkats dig burrows with their long, sharp claws. They fold their ears back so sand cannot get in. They are fast diggers. A meerkat can move its own weight in sand in just seconds.

On the menu

Meerkats dig for food, too. They eat insects, spiders and worms. And scorpions are always on the menu! The scorpion's poison does not hurt meerkats.

Meerkats also eat rodents, lizards, eggs and plants. They spend up to eight hours a day eating. They rarely drink water. They get enough water from the food they eat.

Growing families

Female meerkats give birth one to four times a year. Two to five pups are in each litter. Pups are born hairless and blind. They stay in the burrow for four weeks, drinking their mother's milk. Then they start eating chewed-up food.

The pups huddle to keep warm.
They wrestle and play. Meerkat pups
learn to be part of the mob.

Life in the mob

Up to 30 meerkats live in a mob. They work together to find food and stay safe. The members groom each other to remove ticks and insects. Each mob has a large territory. The mob keeps other meerkats out.

Everyone in the mob has a job to do. Adult meerkats take turns as lookouts. The lookouts find high spots to watch for danger. They warn the mob with a shrill bark when a predator is near.

Babysitters keep pups safe while their mothers hunt. Teachers help pups learn to find food.

Desert dangers

Meerkats face many dangers. Predators such as hawks, snakes and jackals hunt them. Pups can die if they get wet and cold. And humans sometimes damage the areas where meerkats live.

A lookout stands on its hind legs. It uses its tail for balance. The tail is almost as long as its body. Meerkats see very well. They can spot a hawk 300 metres (1,000 feet) away.

Don't mess with the mob! Meerkats team up to chase away cobras, foxes and other small predators. If cornered, meerkats will even attack a jackal. Dust flies as they jump, growl and bite.

When a meerkat gets hurt, the others carry it to the burrow. They feed it and keep it warm. This teamwork is just one reason why meerkats are awesome animals!

Glossary

burrow dig a hole; a burrow can also be a hole in the ground that an animal makes

groom clean and make an animal look neat

litter group of animals born at the same time to one mother

mammal warm–blooded animal with hair or fur

mob group of meerkats that live together

pant breathe quickly with an open mouth; some animals pant to cool off

plains large, flat area of land with few trees

predator animal that hunts other animals for food

territory land on which an animal grazes or hunts for food, and raises its young

Books

Animals in Danger in Africa, Richard and Louise Spilsbury (Raintree, 2013)

Meerkat (A Day in the Life: Desert Animals), Anita Ganeri (Raintree, 2012)

Websites

www.bbc.co.uk/nature/life/Meerkat
Listen to a meerkat growling! Watch videos and find out more interesting facts about this fascinating and fun creature!

www.chesterzoo.org/animals/mammals/meerkats_otters_mongooses/meerkats
Meet the meerkats at Chester Zoo!

Comprehension questions

1. How are meerkat mobs similar to your family? How are they different?

2. Look at all the pictures of meerkat burrows. Describe how they would look in a different part of the world, such as the Alps or Antarctica for example.

3. Where else would a meerkat's coat blend in?

Index